CHRISTIAN CLIP AND COPY GREETING CARDS

by
Vanessa Filkins
and
Rebecca Daniel

illustrated by
Vanessa Filkins

Pam Warden
364-0153
Please do not cut pictures out - copy what you want

Cover by Vanessa Filkins
Shining Star Publications, Copyright © 1991
A Division of Good Apple

ISBN No. 0-86653-631-0

Standardized Subject Code TA ac

Printing No. 987654321

Shining Star Publications
A Division of Good Apple
1204 Buchanan St., Box 299
Carthage, IL 62321-0299

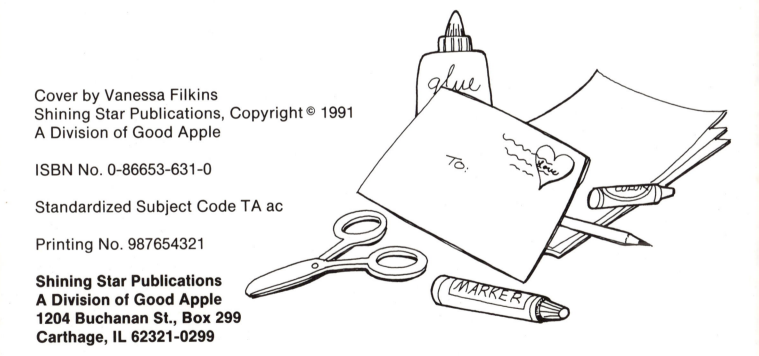

Unless otherwise indicated, the King James Version of the Bible was used in preparing the activities in this book.

DEDICATION

To Virginia, Carol and Nancy:
For some special people who find creative ways
to inspire me to finally finish what I start.

Vanessa

For my special friend who sends me sweet greetings of love.

Rebecca

SS1890

TABLE OF CONTENTS

TO THE TEACHER/PARENT

Put Bible-based greeting cards at your fingertips with this book, *Christian Clip and Copy Greeting Cards.* Each reproducible card found herein is based on scriptures, contains spiritual messages, and is beautifully illustrated.

There are many different ways to use the clip and copy cards. You may just want to color and send the cards yourself. Or, you may want to make enough copies of each card so the children can color and construct the cards, too. The Christmas cards found on pages 7-21 can be used as a nativity display when presented in the proper order. The Easter cards found on pages 23-37 can be used together to tell the Easter story. The Bible hero cards found on pages 39-49 can be an excellent way to culminate units of study on each hero, or they can be used anytime you want to give special recognition to hard-working students.

Children will love the pop-up cards found on pages 51-65. However, very small hands may need help constructing these cards. The Christmas and Easter sticker greeting cards found on pages 67-81 can be used in a variety of ways. Children should be encouraged to use the stickers in any way they choose to create their own unique cards. Stickers can also be colored and attached to small construction paper tags to make nice Christmas gift tags.

Pages 83-93 will provide you with time-saver cards for all occasions. After each member of your class signs the card, you can personalize it by including a flat piece of candy, a bookmark, or any token gift for that special person. Personal messages written inside the card will add to the sentimental value of the gift.

When making greeting cards, use these patterns plus your imagination and invite the children to do the same. Cards may be colored with markers, crayons, waterpaints, etc. Add glitter, cellophane cut-outs, ribbons, stars or stickers. Help your students practice the art of caring by making and giving Bible-based greeting cards.

CHRISTMAS STORY AND EASTER STORY CARDS

The following can be used as individual cards, each with a different scripture. When put together they tell the Christmas story or Easter story.

Materials:

Paper
Crayons
Colored markers
Glue
Glitter
Scissors
Construction paper

Directions:

1. Reproduce one card for each child.
2. Cut out the card along the dotted line.
3. Color the card and decorate with glitter if desired.
4. Fold the card in half.
5. Write the suggested greeting inside the card or let children fill in their own greetings.

Card Variation:

Turn the eight individual cards into one Christmas or Easter story greeting. Reproduce one of each card and cut out the right side only of each card. Color and decorate each picture as desired. Cut out a sheet of construction paper 7½" x 10". Fold the construction paper in half and insert cards in the proper order and staple through all layers along the left side. Write your own special message and decorate the cover as desired.

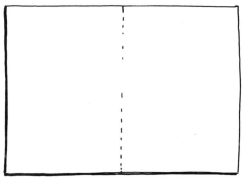

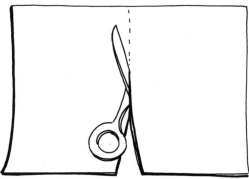

Use this greeting as a gift or card for someone very special.

SS1890

SS1890

"And the angel said unto her, Fear not, Mary: . . .thou shalt. . .bring forth a son, and shalt call his name JESUS." Luke 1:30,31

CHRISTMAS—ANGEL
Suggested Greeting: HAPPY CHRISTMAS

SS1890

SS1890

"And Joseph also went up from Galilee, . .unto the city. . .which is called Bethle-hem; . . .To be taxed with Mary. . .being great with child."

Luke 2:4,5

CHRISTMAS—JOSEPH AND MARY
Suggested Greeting: WARM HOLIDAY GREETINGS

Shining Star Publications, Copyright © 1991, A Division of Good Apple

9

SS1890

SS1890

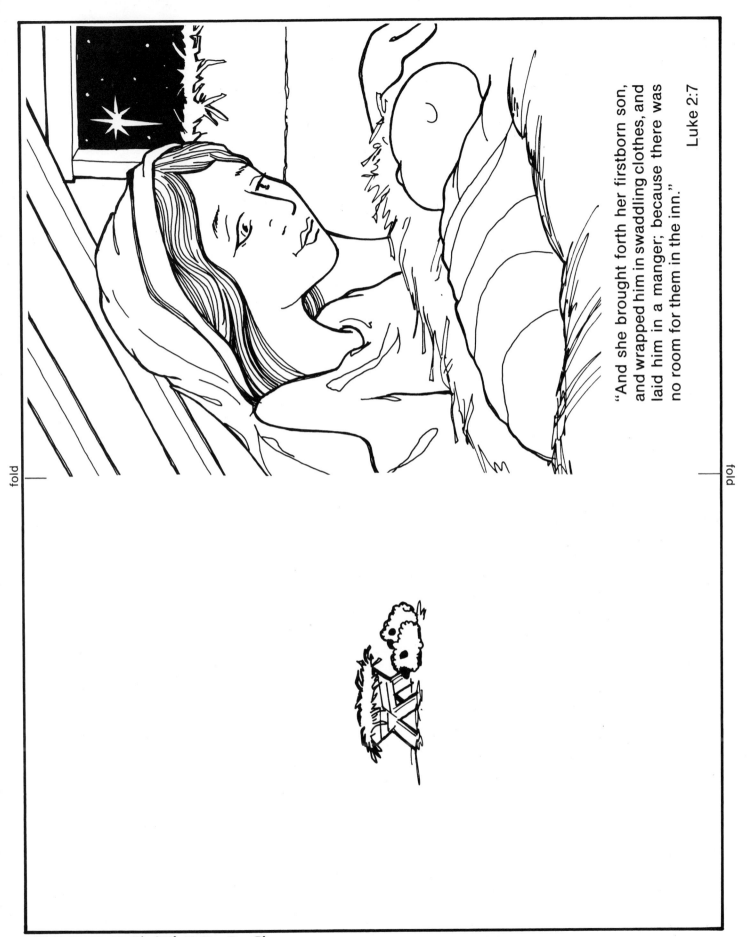

"And she brought forth her firstborn son, and wrapped him in swaddling clothes, and laid him in a manger; because there was no room for them in the inn."

Luke 2:7

CHRISTMAS—MARY AND JESUS
Suggested Greeting: THERE WAS NO ROOM IN THE INN

Shining Star Publications, Copyright © 1991, A Division of Good Apple

SS1890

SS1890

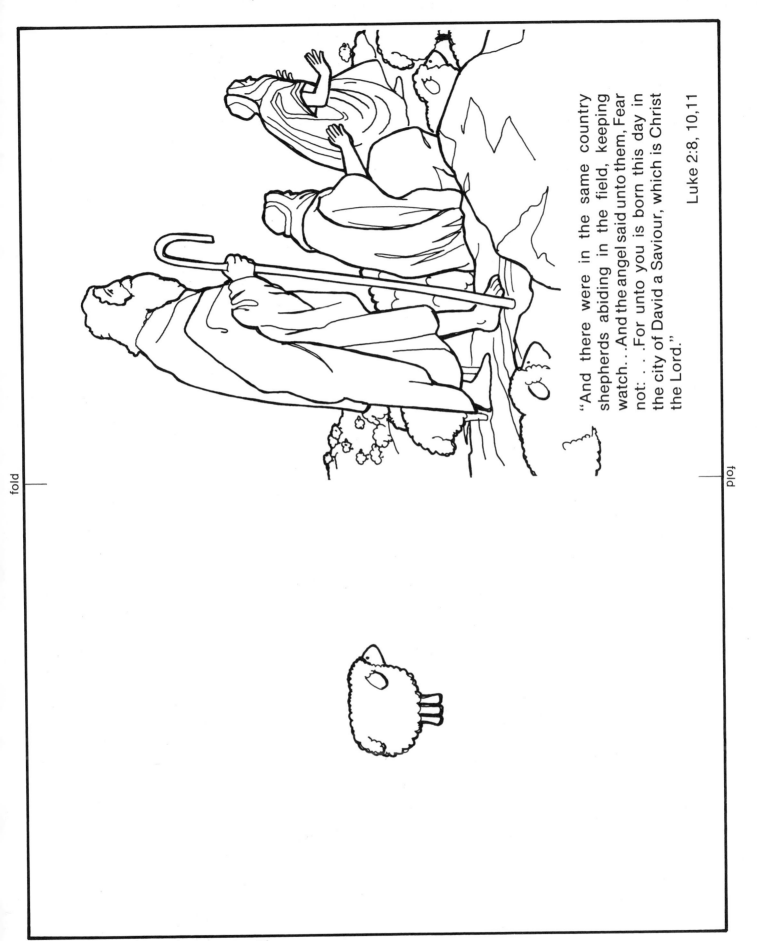

"And there were in the same country shepherds abiding in the field, keeping watch...And the angel said unto them, Fear not: . . .For unto you is born this day in the city of David a Saviour, which is Christ the Lord."

Luke 2:8, 10,11

CHRISTMAS—SHEPHERDS
Suggested Greeting: A SAVIOUR WAS BORN

Shining Star Publications, Copyright © 1991, A Division of Good Apple

SS1890

SS1890

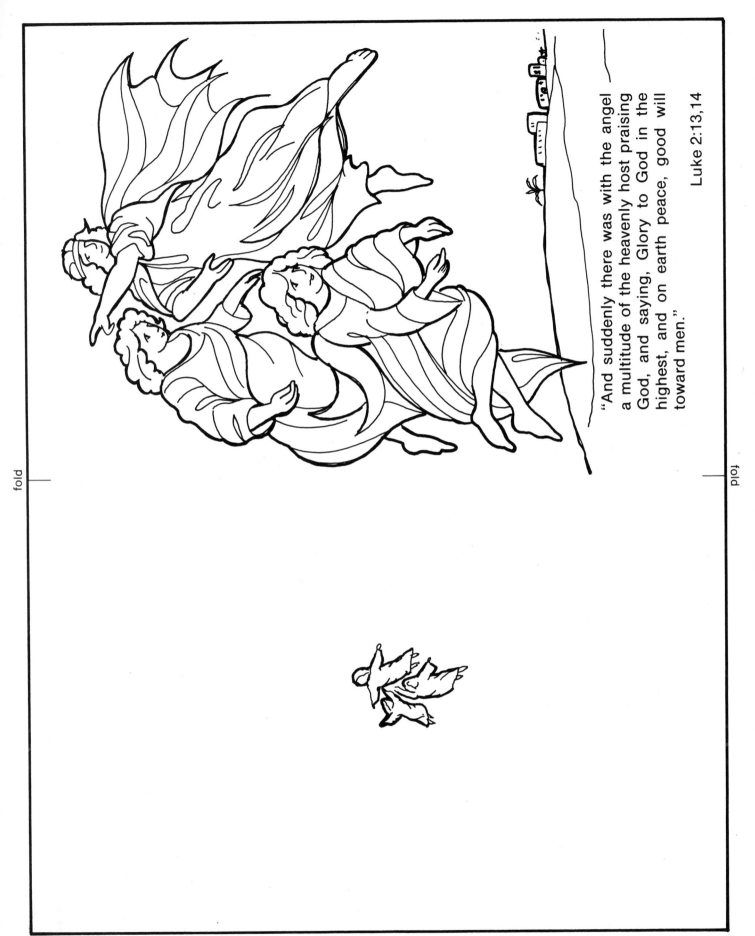

"And suddenly there was with the angel a multitude of the heavenly host praising God, and saying, Glory to God in the highest, and on earth peace, good will toward men."

Luke 2:13,14

CHRISTMAS—ANGELS OVER THE STABLE
Suggested Greeting: GLORY TO GOD IN THE HIGHEST

SS1890

SS1890

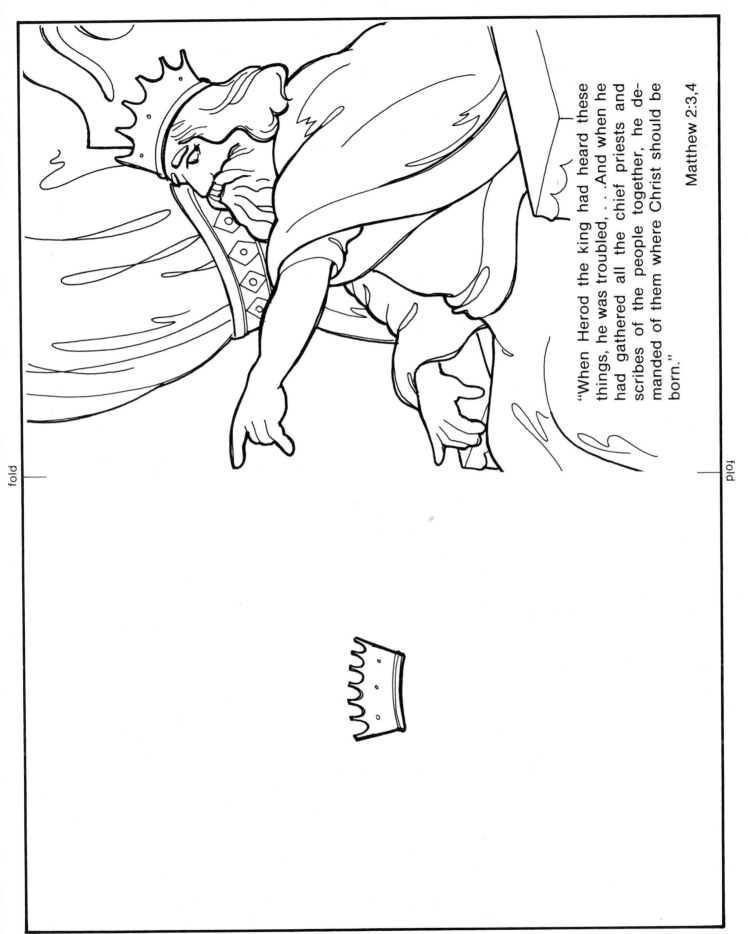

"When Herod the king had heard these things, he was troubled, . . .And when he had gathered all the chief priests and scribes of the people together, he demanded of them where Christ should be born."

Matthew 2:3,4

fold

fold

CHRISTMAS—KING HEROD
Suggested Greeting: PEACE ON EARTH

Shining Star Publications, Copyright © 1991, A Division of Good Apple

SS1890

SS1890

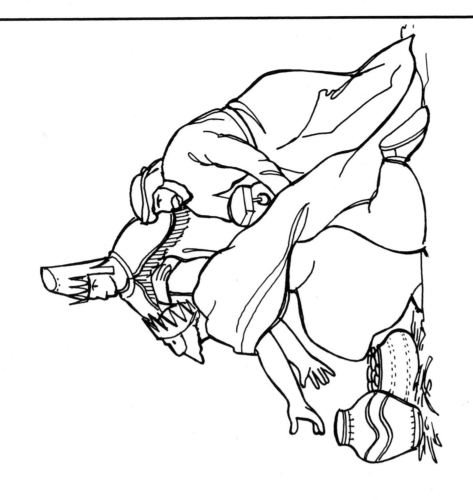

"And when they were come into the house, they saw the young child with Mary his mother, and fell down, and worshipped him: and when they had opened their treasures, they presented unto him gifts; gold, and frankincense, and myrrh."

Matthew 2:11

CHRISTMAS—WISE MEN
Suggested Greeting: EXCEEDING GREAT JOY

SS1890

SS1890

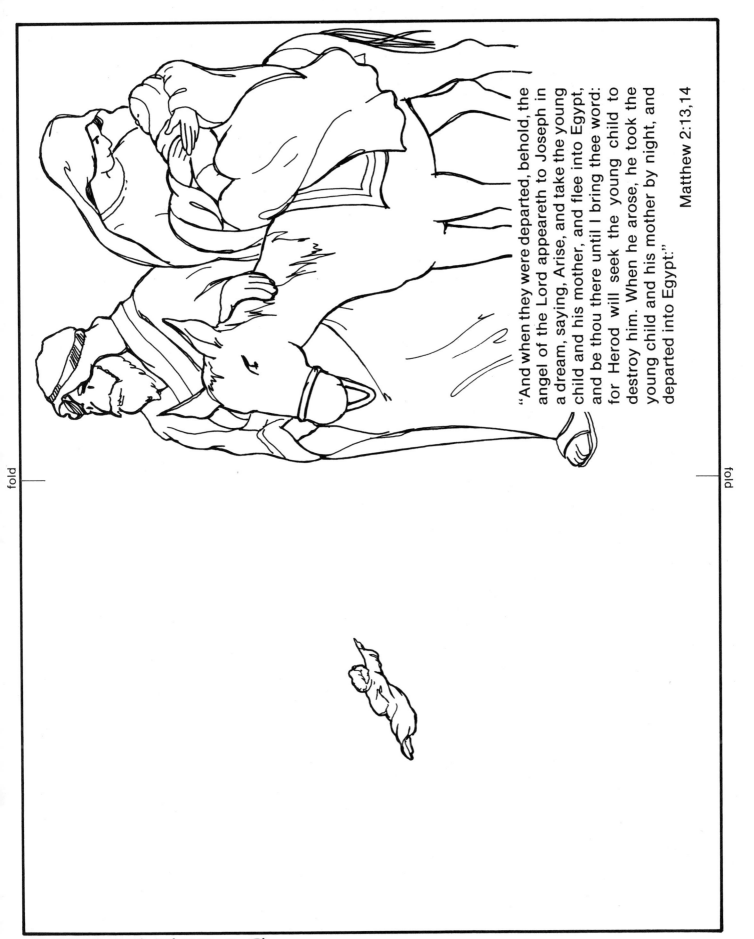

"And when they were departed, behold, the angel of the Lord appeareth to Joseph in a dream, saying, Arise, and take the young child and his mother, and flee into Egypt, and be thou there until I bring thee word: for Herod will seek the young child to destroy him. When he arose, he took the young child and his mother by night, and departed into Egypt." Matthew 2:13,14

fold

fold

CHRISTMAS—JOSEPH, MARY AND JESUS
Suggested Greeting: GOOD WILL TOWARD ALL MEN

SS1890

22

SS1890

"...Blessed is he that cometh in the name of the Lord; Hosanna in the highest."
Matthew 21:9

EASTER—JESUS' ENTRY
Suggested Greeting: JESUS CAME

23

SS1890

"And the blind and the lame came to him in the temple; and he healed them." Matthew 21:14

fold

fold

EASTER—HEALING IN THE TEMPLE

Suggested Greeting: LOVE YOUR NEIGHBOR

SS1890

SS1890

"Now when the even was come, he sat down with the twelve." Matthew 26:20

fold

fold

EASTER—LAST SUPPER
Suggested Greeting: AND THEN THEY SANG

SS1890

SS1890

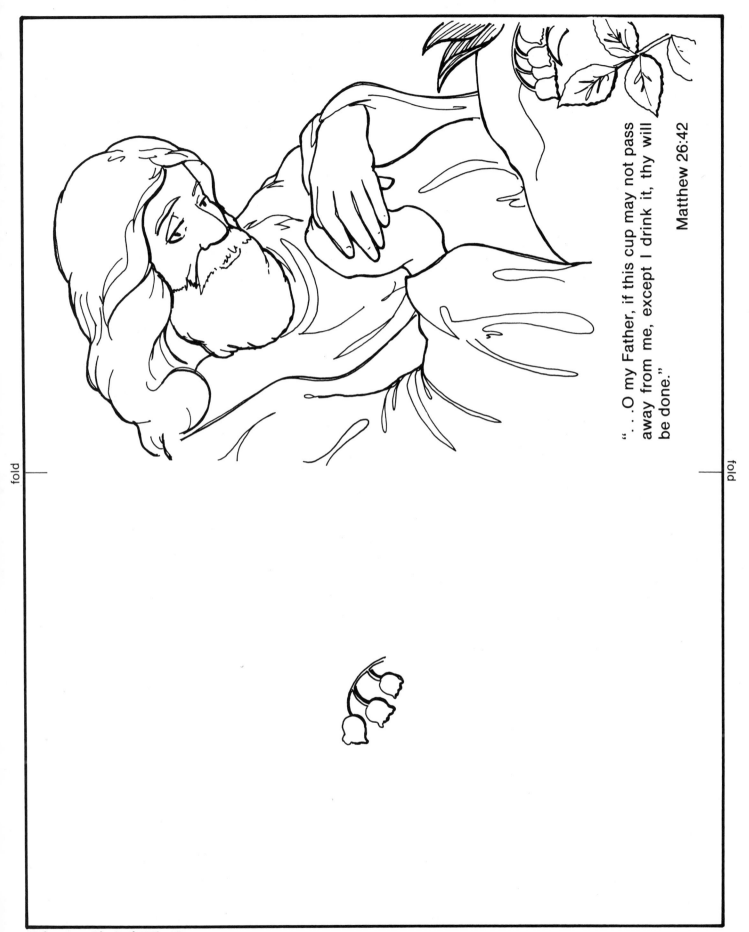

"...O my Father, if this cup may not pass away from me, except I drink it, thy will be done."

Matthew 26:42

EASTER—PRAYING IN THE GARDEN

Suggested Greeting: HE PRAYED

SS1890

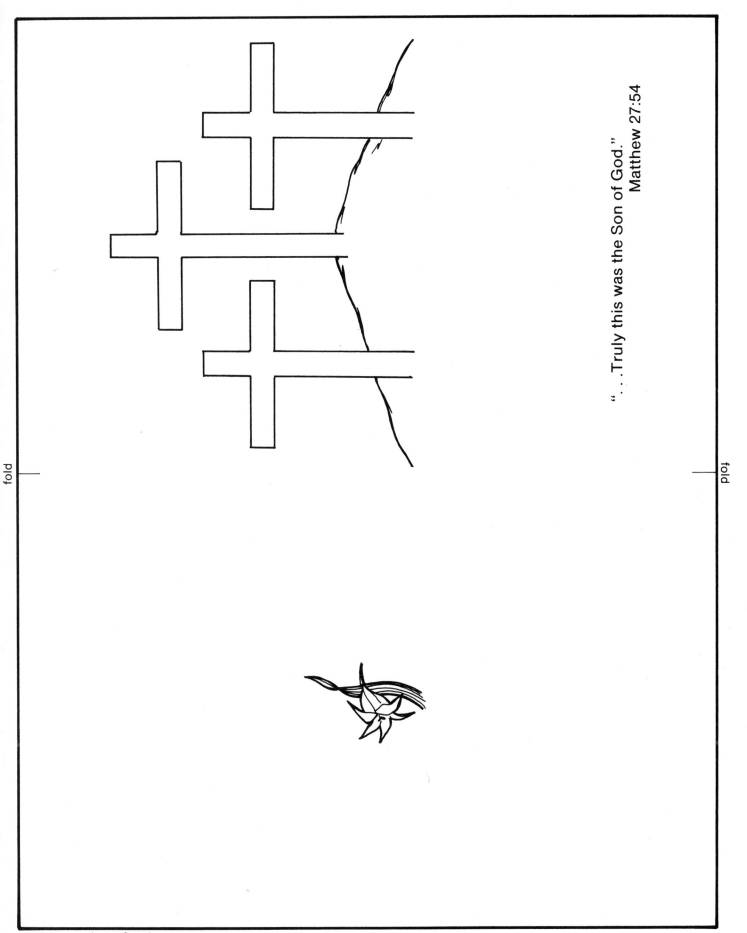

"...Truly this was the Son of God."
Matthew 27:54

EASTER—JESUS IS CRUCIFIED
Suggested Greeting: JESUS DIED FOR US

31

SS1890

32

SS1890

"...for the angel of the Lord descended from heaven, and came and rolled back the stone from the door, and sat upon it."
Matthew 28:2

EASTER—ANGEL
Suggested Greeting: IT BEGAN AT DAWN

Shining Star Publications, Copyright © 1991, A Division of Good Apple

SS1890

34

SS1890

"He is not here: for he is risen, as he said. . . ." Matthew 28:6

EASTER—WOMEN AT TOMB
Suggested Greeting: JESUS LIVES!

SS1890

SS1890

"So then after the Lord had spoken unto them, he was received up into heaven, and sat on the right hand of God." Mark 16:19

EASTER—HIS ASCENSION
Suggested Greeting: AMEN

SS1890

SS1890

BIBLE HERO—MOSES

When God appeared to Moses from the burning bush, Moses was filled with doubt. He didn't think he was the right person to lead his people. You can read all about how God reassured Moses by turning to Exodus in your Bible and reading chapters seven through ten.

YOU ARE VERY SPECIAL

"And God said unto Moses, I AM THAT I AM: . . ." Exodus 3:14

Can you find the path through the maze that passes each of the nine plagues in the order in which they occurred? To check your answer, read Exodus 7:20–10:29.

START →

FINISH

SS1890

SS1890

BIBLE HERO—JOSHUA

Joshua led his people on the march around Jericho for seven days. As the Lord promised, on the seventh day the wall fell down flat. Read about this adventure in the sixth chapter of Joshua.

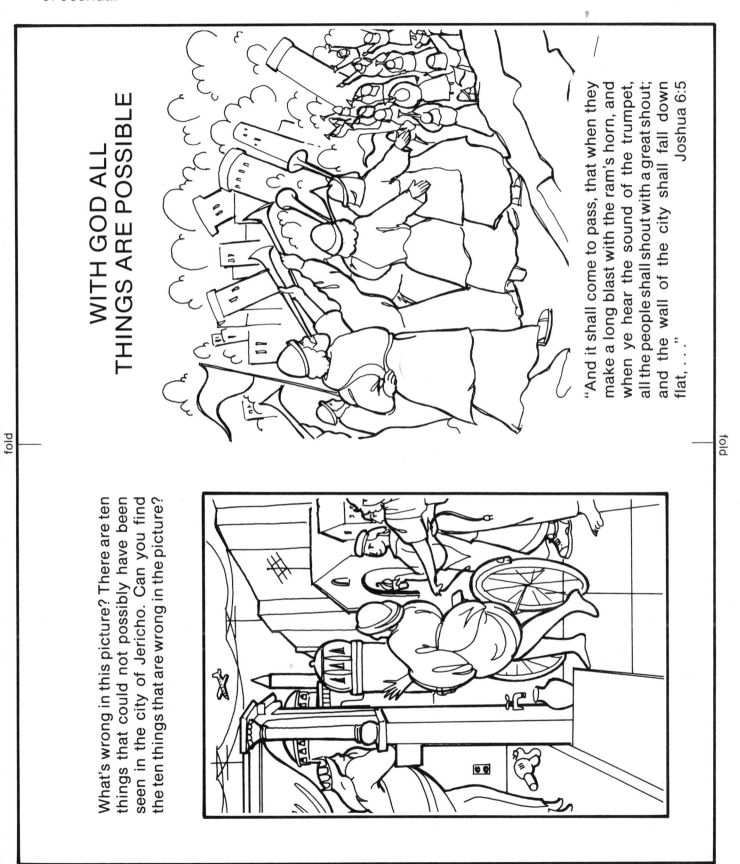

WITH GOD ALL
THINGS ARE POSSIBLE

"And it shall come to pass, that when they make a long blast with the ram's horn, and when ye hear the sound of the trumpet, all the people shall shout with a great shout; and the wall of the city shall fall down flat, ..." Joshua 6:5

What's wrong in this picture? There are ten things that could not possibly have been seen in the city of Jericho. Can you find the ten things that are wrong in the picture?

SS1890

BIBLE HERO—NOAH

Noah listened to God and did as God told him. Although his neighbors laughed at him, Noah continued to labor until he completed the ark. When the rains began, Noah's family and the animals were safely on the ark.

HAPPY DAY!

"And Noah did according unto all that the Lord commanded him." Genesis 7:5

Hidden in the picture are ten animals. Can you find them?

SS1890

SS1890

BIBLE HERO—JOSEPH

Joseph dreamed of the future and told his brothers about his dreams. Joseph's dreams made his brothers angry. One day young Joseph was sold into slavery by his brothers. Find out what happened to Joseph by reading Genesis 37.

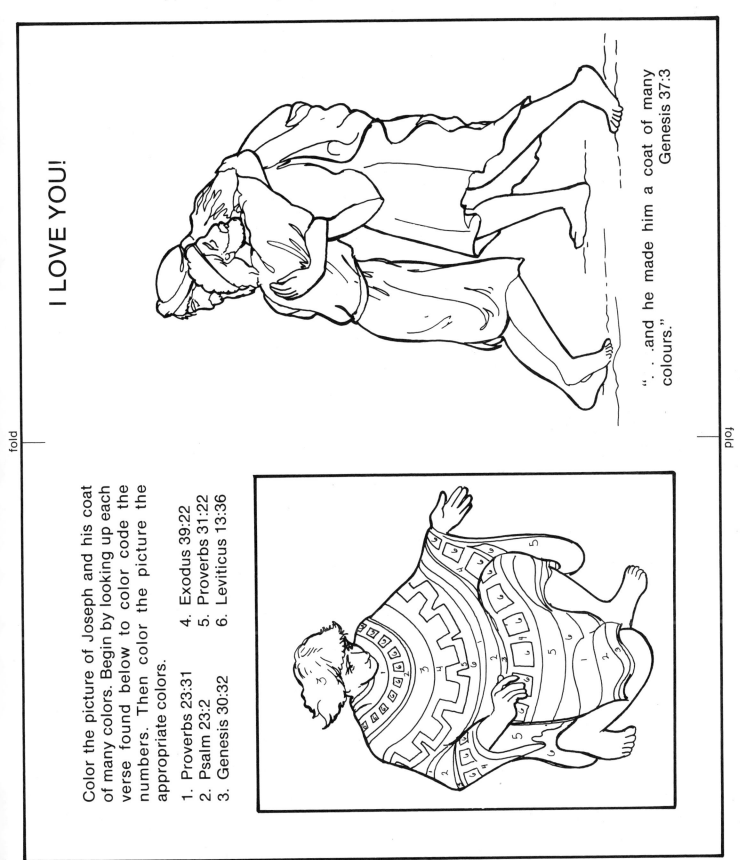

I LOVE YOU!

"...and he made him a coat of many colours." Genesis 37:3

Color the picture of Joseph and his coat of many colors. Begin by looking up each verse found below to color code the numbers. Then color the picture the appropriate colors.

1. Proverbs 23:31
2. Psalm 23:2
3. Genesis 30:32
4. Exodus 39:22
5. Proverbs 31:22
6. Leviticus 13:36

SS1890

SS1890

BIBLE HERO—DANIEL

Daniel was put in a den of lions because of his faith in God. The Lord closed the mouths of the lions so they would not harm Daniel. Read all about Daniel and his friends, Shadrach, Meschach and Abed-nego in the book of Daniel.

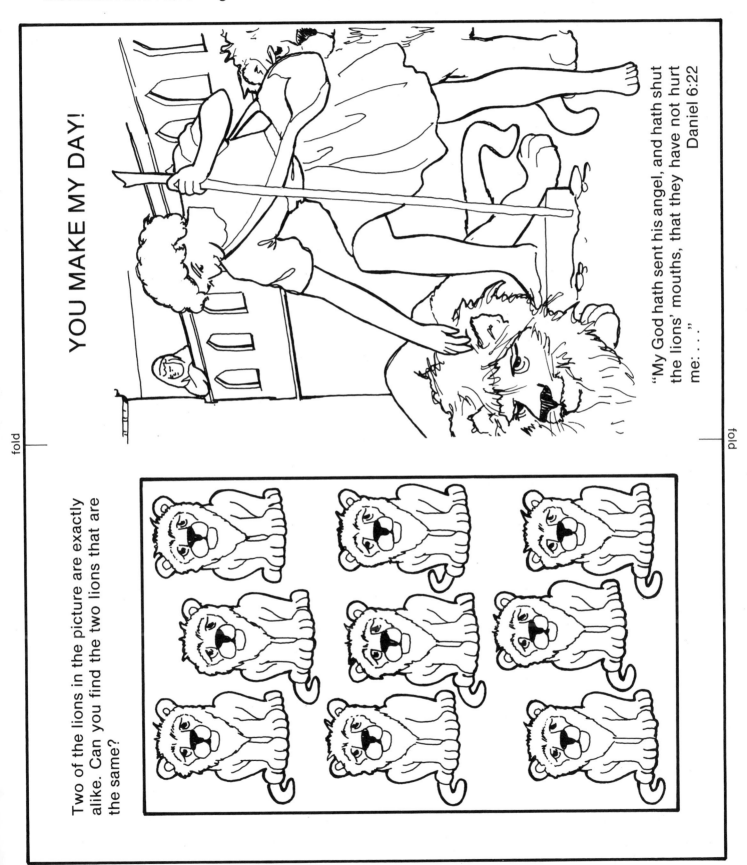

YOU MAKE MY DAY!

"My God hath sent his angel, and hath shut the lions' mouths, that they have not hurt me: . . ."
Daniel 6:22

Two of the lions in the picture are exactly alike. Can you find the two lions that are the same?

SS1890

BIBLE HERO—DAVID

For forty days Goliath had challenged the Israelites. None of the soldiers would accept the challenge. Only David, the young shepherd, was brave enough to meet the giant. What happened when the young shepherd boy offered to meet the giant? What did the King offer David? Why were David's brothers angry with him? You can find out all about David. His story is told in I Samuel chapters 16 and 17.

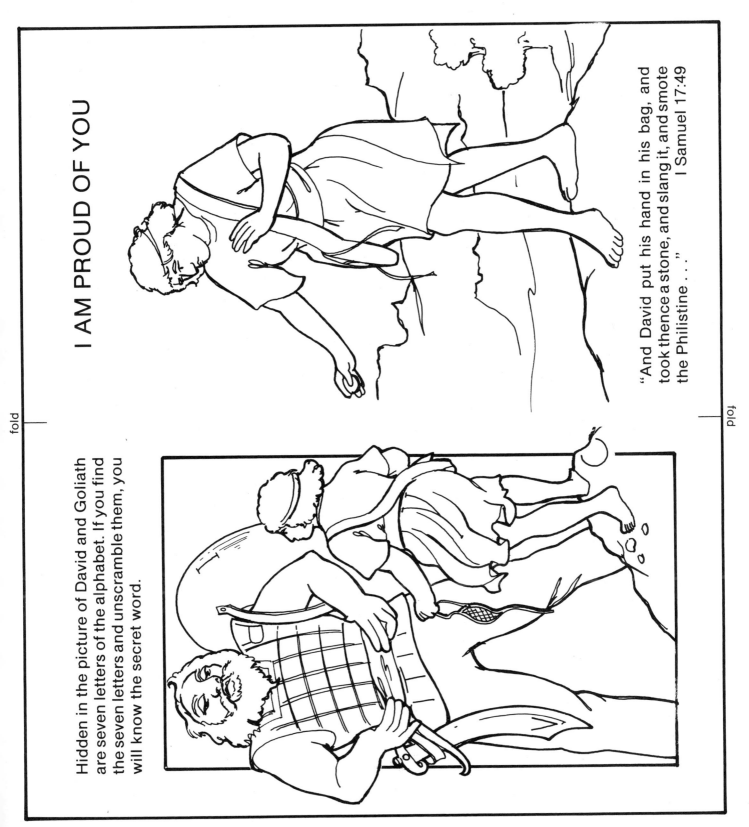

I AM PROUD OF YOU

"And David put his hand in his bag, and took thence a stone, and slang it, and smote the Philistine . . ."
I Samuel 17:49

Hidden in the picture of David and Goliath are seven letters of the alphabet. If you find the seven letters and unscramble them, you will know the secret word.

fold

fold

Shining Star Publications, Copyright © 1991, A Division of Good Apple

SS1890

SS1890

POP-UP—JONAH

Fold where indicated. Cut dashed line to form mouth flap. Glue half of tab to back of Jonah. Position the other half of Jonah tab on back panel under mouth flap and glue in place. Write your own greeting on inside of mouth flap.

fold

fold

fold

SS1890

SS1890

Noah's ark forms a pocket that can be filled with freestanding animals. Cut door flap along dashed lines. Fold. Glue along side edges as indicated. When door is opened, Noah can be seen. Write verse of your choice on inside of door flap. Glue patterns to heavy paper or lightweight poster board. Glue stands to the back of ark and animals.

POP-UP—NOAH

glue Noah under flap

glue along edge

glue along edge

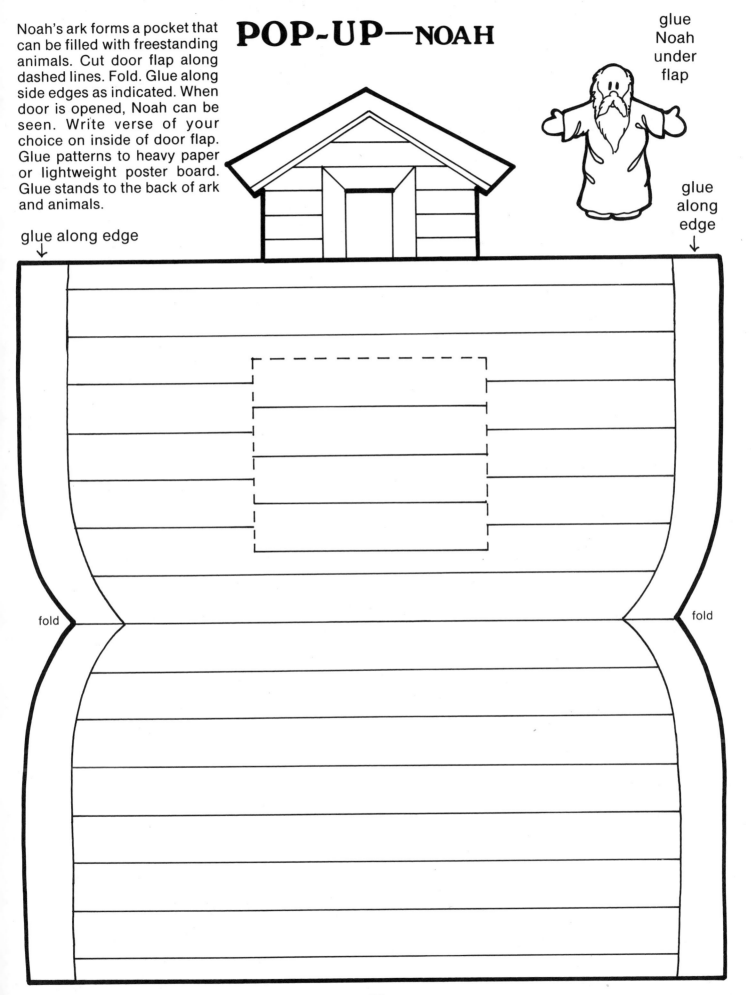

fold

fold

SS1890

SS1890

ANIMAL PATTERNS

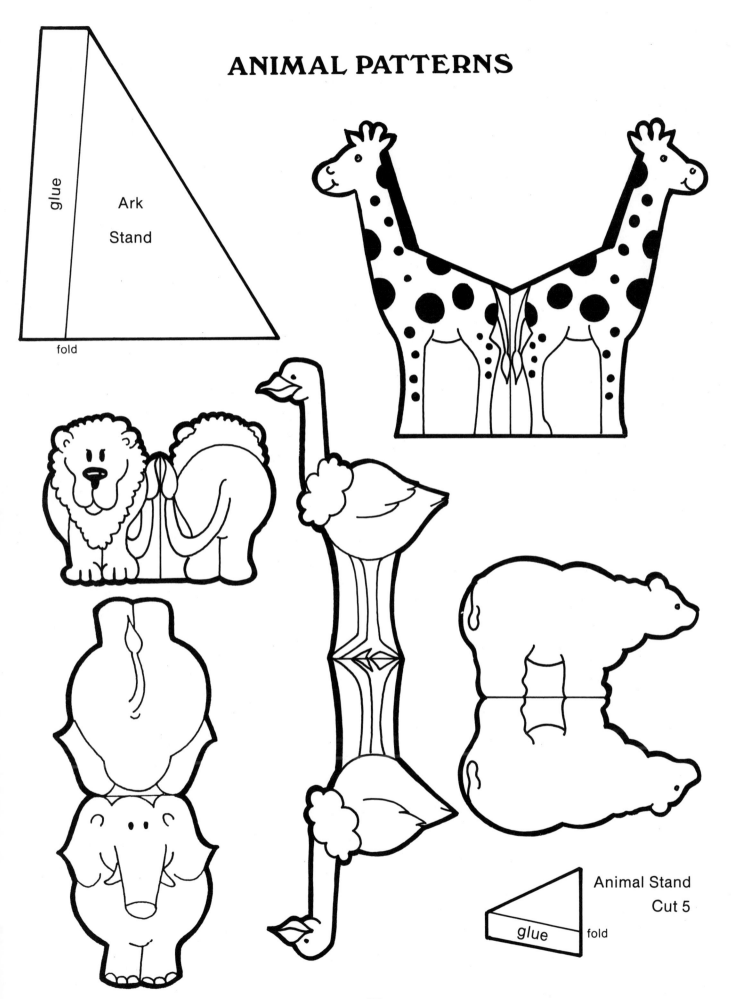

glue

Ark
Stand

fold

Animal Stand
Cut 5

glue fold

SS1890

SS1890

POP-UP—RED SEA

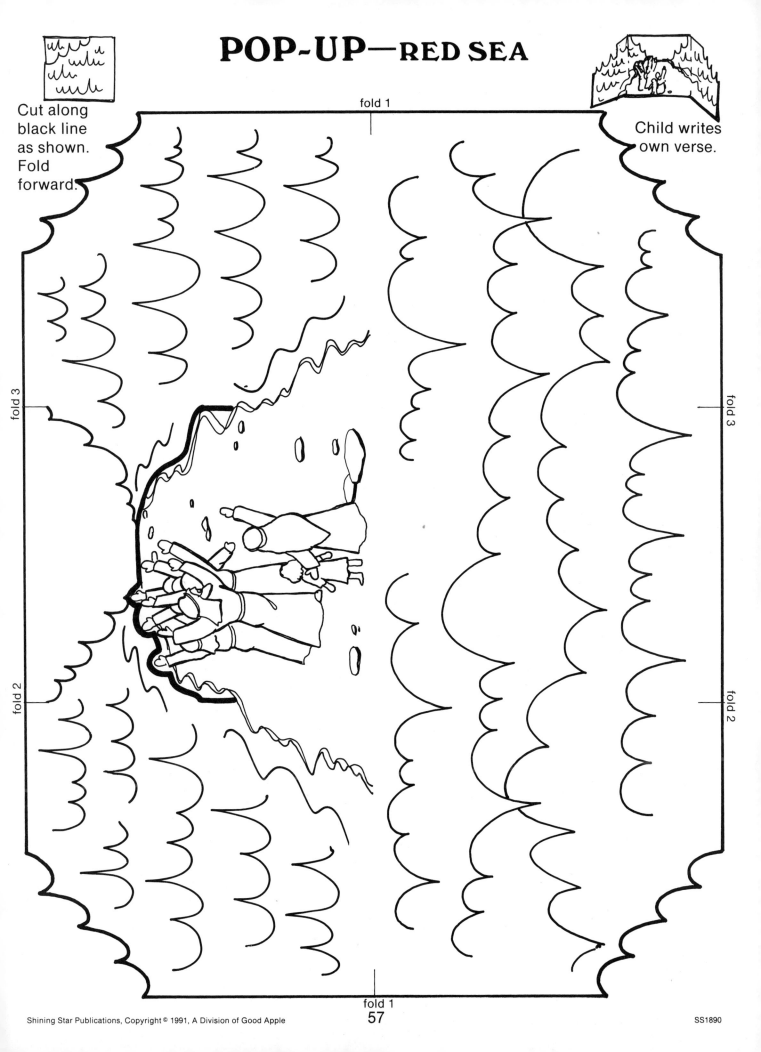

fold 1

Cut along
black line
as shown.
Fold
forward.

Child writes
own verse.

fold 3

fold 3

fold 2

fold 2

SS1890

POP-UP—NATIVITY

This greeting card folds flat for easy mailing. Include an instruction card with each greeting card. Write your very own special message on the outside panels of the card.

fold and glue

fold and glue

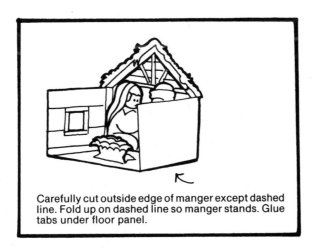

Carefully cut outside edge of manger except dashed line. Fold up on dashed line so manger stands. Glue tabs under floor panel.

SS1890

SS1890

POP-UP—WINDOW AND FLOWERS

Fold as illustrated. Cut slots for flower tabs.
Apple glue to tabs and insert into slots.
Write verse of choice above flowers.

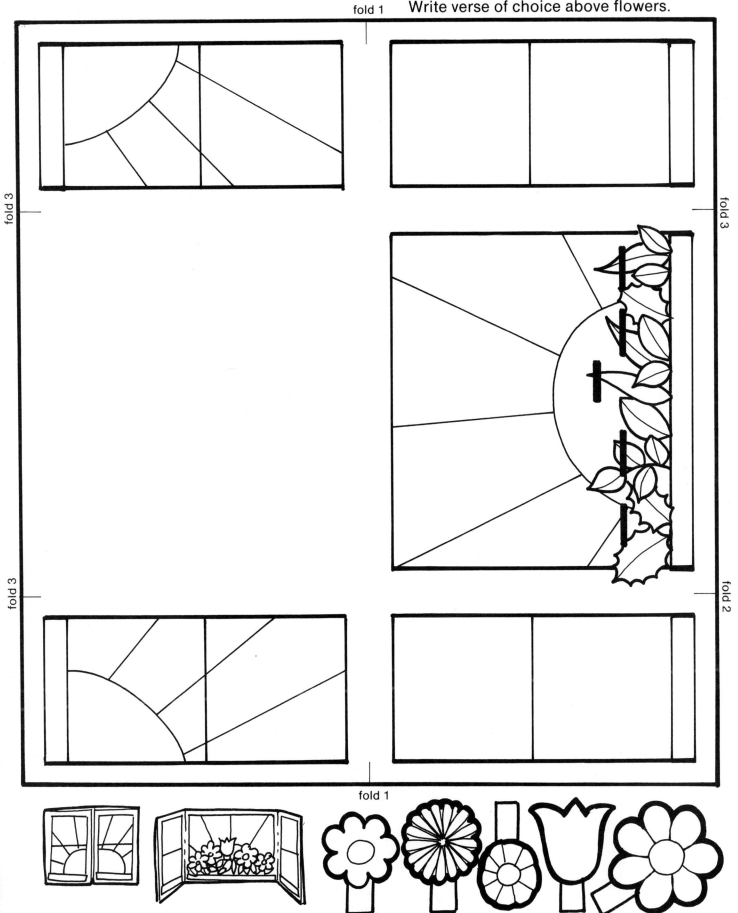

POP-UP—HOUSE WITH PHOTO

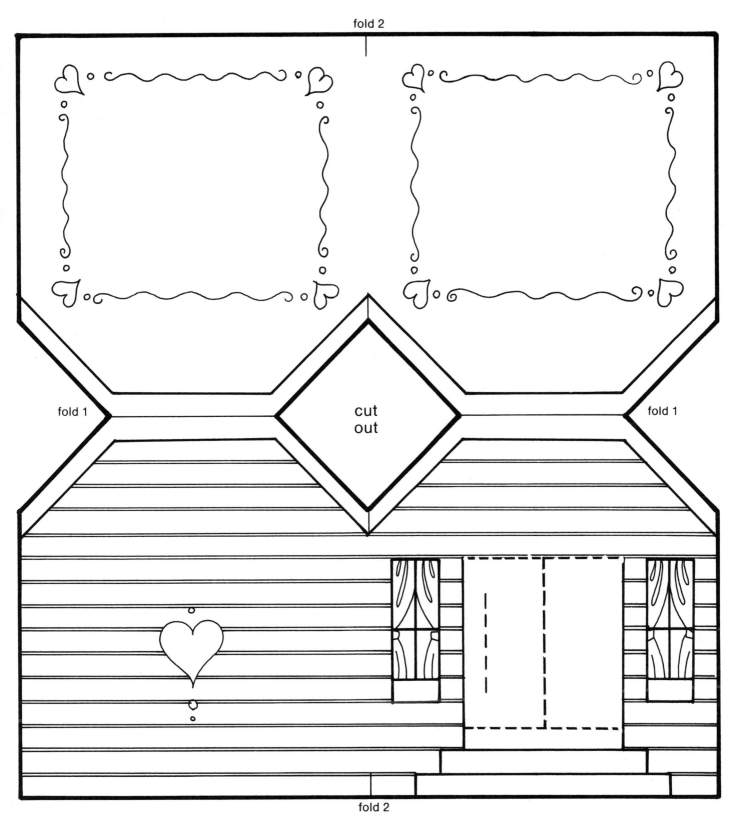

fold 2

fold 1

cut out

fold 1

fold 2

Color, cut and fold card and heart as indicated. Cut dashed lines on door. Glue right half of heart to right side of door lining up the tab even with the tab slot. Close door by sliding tab into slot. Tape or glue photo directly behind open door. Write verse of choice inside house.

SS1890

SS1890

POP-UP—CANDLE BOOKMARK

1. Color and cut out patterns.
2. Fold envelope along fold lines.
3. Tape sides together to close.
4. Write Bible verse or message on card and envelope.
5. Put bookmark in envelope.

SS1890

SS1890

CHRISTMAS STICKER GREETING
MANGER

fold

fold

SS1890

SS1890

CHRISTMAS STICKER GREETING
NIGHT SCENE

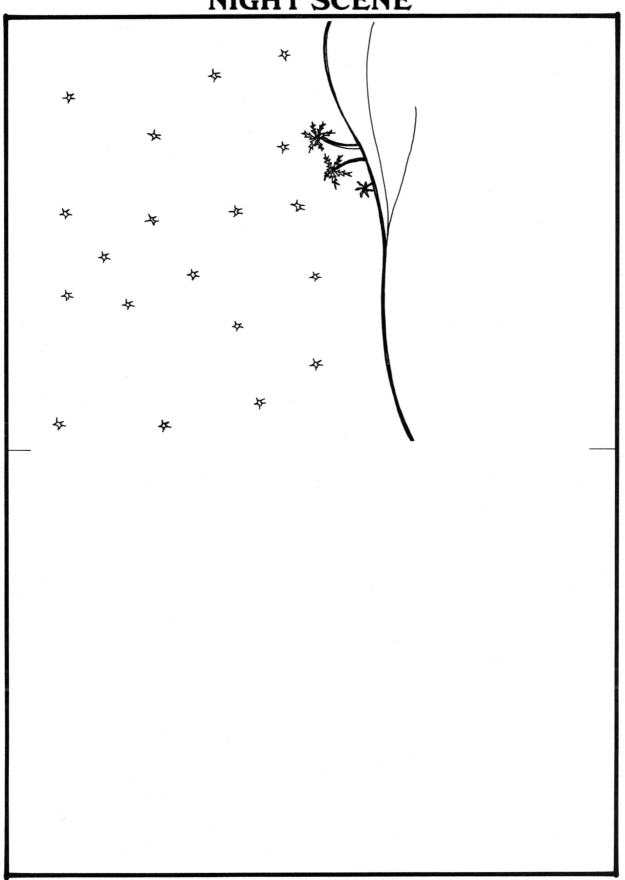

SS1890

SS1890

STICKERS

SS1890

SS1890

STICKERS

SS1890

EASTER STICKER GREETING
JERUSALEM

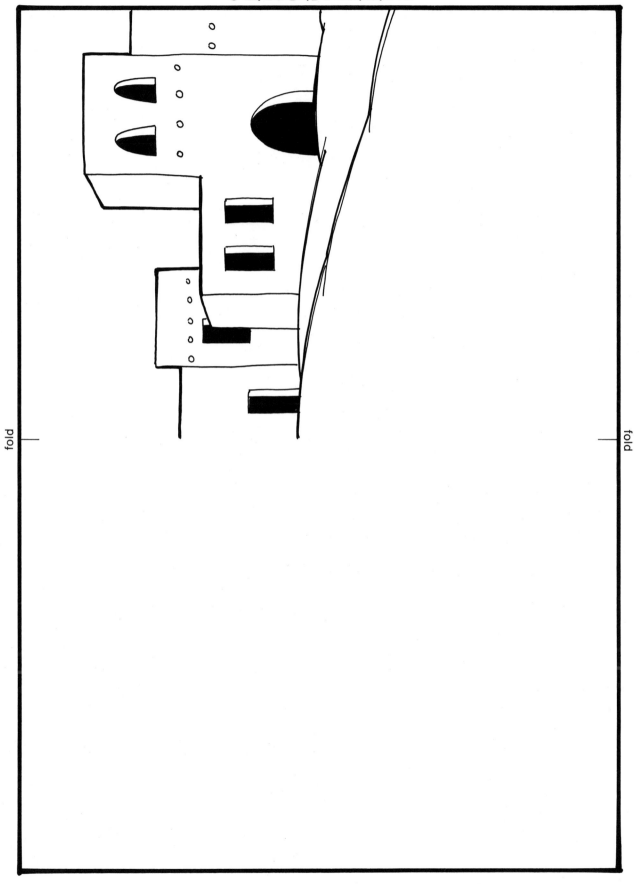

fold

fold

75

SS1890

SS1890

EASTER STICKER GREETING
THE TOMB

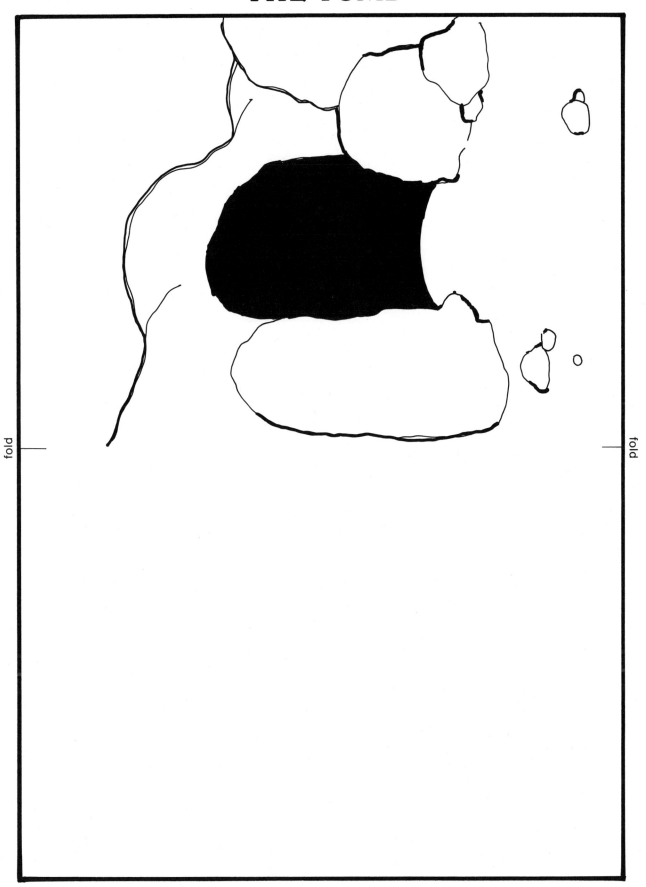

fold

fold

SS1890

SS1890

STICKERS

SS1890

SS1890

STICKERS

SS1890

SS1890

HAPPY BIRTHDAY (BOY)

Glue or draw appropriate number of candles on cake using pattern provided. Bend tabs back on "Happy Birthday" and glue to inside edge of card.

83

SS1890

SS1890

HAPPY BIRTHDAY (GIRL)

fold 2

fold 1

fold 1

Holy Bible

love

A Special Birthday Wish for You

fold 2

Add your own message in the space provided.

SS1890

HOORAY FOR LOST TOOTH

SS1890

SS1890

SS1890

WE MISSED YOU

Color, cut and fold as indicated. Draw and write an additional greeting on the front.

fold 1

fold 2

fold 2

fold 1

SS1890

WE WILL MISS YOU

Color, cut and fold. Write the name of the person leaving in the heart. Add your own message inside.

fold

fold

We Will Miss You

Name

SS1890

SS1890

ANSWER KEY

Bible Hero—Moses Page 39

blood
frogs
gnats
flies
livestock
foils
hail
locust
darkness

Bible Hero—Joshua Page 41
TV antenna
ice cream cone
bike
extension cord
water spigot
tennis shoe
power lines
electric outlet
hair dryer
airplane

Bible Hero—Noah Page 43

Bible Hero—Joseph Page 45
1-red
2-green
3-brown
4-blue
5-purple
6-yellow

Bible Hero—Daniel Page 47

Bible Hero—David Page 49

Secret word: victory

 SS1890

SS1890